INTRODUCTION

Welcome back to FastTrack™!

Hope you enjoyed Bass 1 and are ready to play some hits. Have you and your friends formed a band? Or do you feel like soloing with the audio? Either way, make sure you're turned up loud…it's time to jam!

The eight songs in this book appear in the order of their difficulty. With the knowledge you already have, you're ready to play all of these songs. But it's still important to remember the three Ps: **patience**, **practice** and **pace yourself**.

As with Bass 1, don't try to bite off more than you can chew. If your fingers hurt, take some time off. If you get frustrated, put down your bass, relax and just listen to the audio. If you forget a note position or rhythmic value, go back and learn it. If you're doing fine, think about charging admission.

CONTENTS

ABOUT THE AUDIO

Again, you get audio with the book! Each song in the book is included, so you can hear how it sounds and play along when you're ready.

Each audio example is preceded by one measure of "clicks" to indicate the tempo and meter. Pan right to hear the bass part emphasized. Pan left to hear the accompaniment emphasized.

ISBN 978-0-7935-7415-5

HAL•LEONARD®
CORPORATION
7777 W. BLUEMOUND RD. P.O. BOX 13819 MILWAUKEE, WI 53213

Visit Hal Leonard online at
www.halleonard.com

LEARN SOMETHING NEW EACH DAY

We know you're eager to play, but first you need to learn a few new things. We'll make it brief—only two pages...

Melody and Lyrics

All of the melody lines and lyrics to these great songs are included for your musical pleasure (and benefit). These are shown on an extra musical staff, which we added above your part.

Unfortunately, bass players never (OK, rarely) play the melody, but this added vocal line will help you follow the song more easily as you play your part.

And whether you have a singer in the band or decide to carry the tune yourself, this new staff is your key to adding some vocals to your tunes.

Endings

Several of the songs have some interesting little symbols that you must understand before playing. Each of these symbols represents a different type of ending.

1st and 2nd Endings

You know these from *Bass 1* (the brackets with numbers):

REMINDER: Simply play the song through to the first ending, repeat back to the first repeat sign, or beginning of the song (whichever is the case). Play through the song again, but skip the first ending and play the second ending.

D.S. al Coda

When you see these words, go back and repeat from this symbol: 𝄋

Play until you see the words *"To Coda"* then skip to the Coda, indicated by this symbol: 𝄌

Now just finish the song.a
Play until you see the words *"To Coda"* then skip to the Coda, indicated by this symbol: 𝄌

Now just finish the song.

Song Structure

Most songs have different sections, which might be recognizable by any or all of the following:

 INTRODUCTION (or "intro"): This is a short section at the beginning that (you guessed it again!) "introduces" the song to the listeners.

 VERSES: One of the main sections of the song is the **verse**. There will usually be several verses, all with the same music but each with different lyrics.

 CHORUS: Perhaps the most memorable section of a song is the **chorus**. Again, there might be several choruses, but each chorus will often have the same lyrics and music.

 BRIDGE: This section makes a transition from one part of a song to the next. For example, you may find a bridge between the chorus and next verse.

 SOLOS: Sometimes solos are played over the verse or chorus structure, but in some songs the solo section has its own structure. This is your time to stand back and show your support for the soloist.

 OUTRO: Similar to the "intro," this section brings the song to an end.

That's about it! Enjoy the music...

① You Really Got Me

Words and Music by Ray Davies

Lyrics:
1. Girl, you real-ly got me go-in'. You got me so I don't know what I'm do-in'.
2. See, don't ev-er set me free. I al-ways wan-na be by your side.

Yeah, you real-ly

real-ly got me.

Guitar Solo

Wild Thing

Words and Music by Chip Taylor

Verse

1. Wild Thing, I _____ think I love _ you, but I wan - na know_
2. Wild Thing, I _____ think you move _ me, but I wan - na know_

_____ for sure. _ Come on and hold me tight.
_____ for sure. _ Come on and hold me tight.

Interlude

I love you.
you move me.

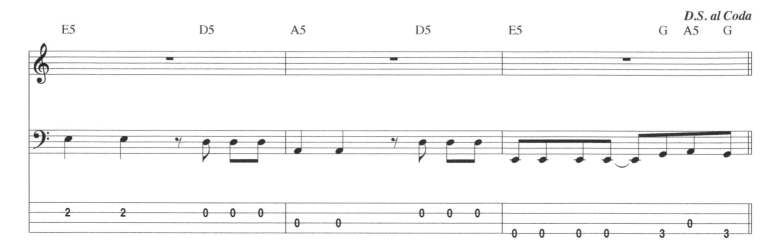

Coda

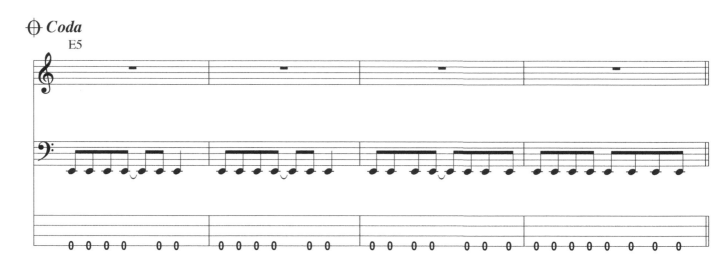

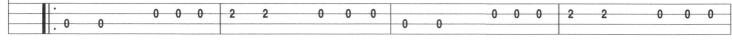

Outro–Chorus

Wild Thing,   you make my heart sing.   You make ev -

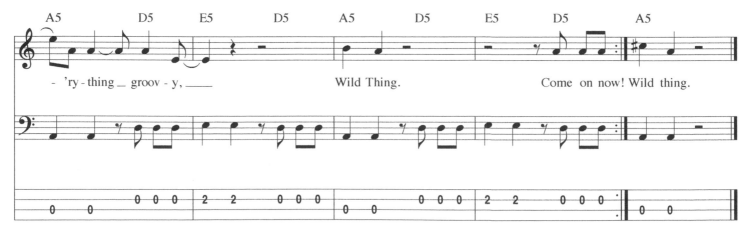

- 'ry - thing _ groov - y, ____   Wild Thing.   Come on now! Wild thing.

I Want to Hold Your Hand

Words and Music by John Lennon and Paul McCartney

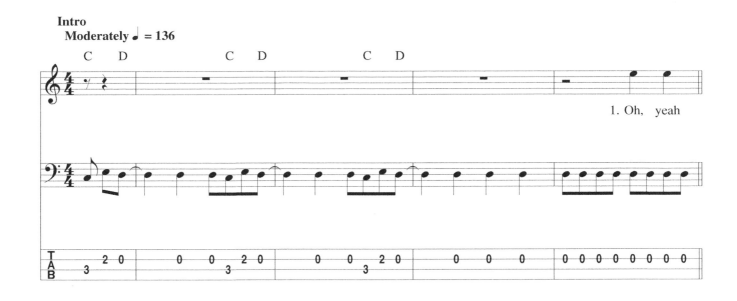

Chorus

I want to hold your hand _____ I want to hold your _

Verse

hand.   2. Oh,   please ___   say to   me ___   you'll let me be your
            you ___   got that some - thing,   I think you'll un - der -

man.   And   please ___   say to   me ___   you'll let me hold your hand._
stand.   When I ___   say that some - thing,   I want to hold your hand._

Chorus

Now let me hold your hand _____
I want to hold your hand _____
I want to hold your ___

I want to hold your hand _____
I want to hold your ___

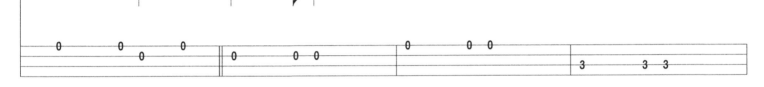

Bridge

hand.
hand.

And when I touch you I feel hap-py in -

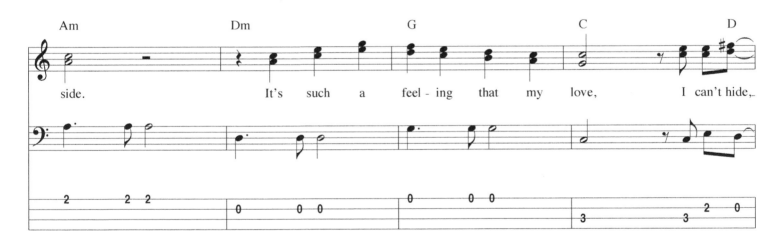

side. It's such a feel-ing that my love, I can't hide, ___

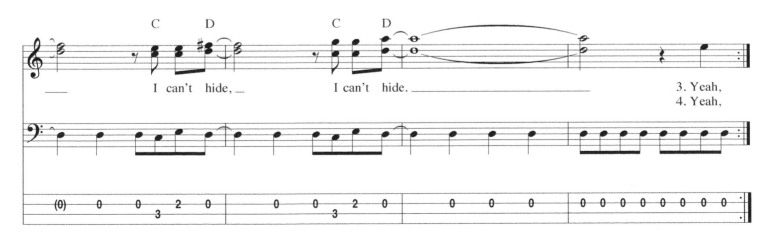

___ I can't hide, ___ I can't hide. _____

3. Yeah,
4. Yeah,

Verse

you ___ got that some - thing, I think you'll un - der - stand. When

I ___ feel that some - thing I want to hold your hand. __

Outro–Chorus

I want to hold your hand. _____ I want to hold your

hand I want to hold your hand. _____

Wonderful Tonight

Words and Music by Eric Clapton

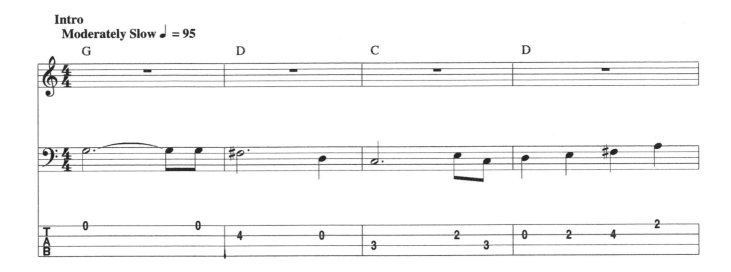

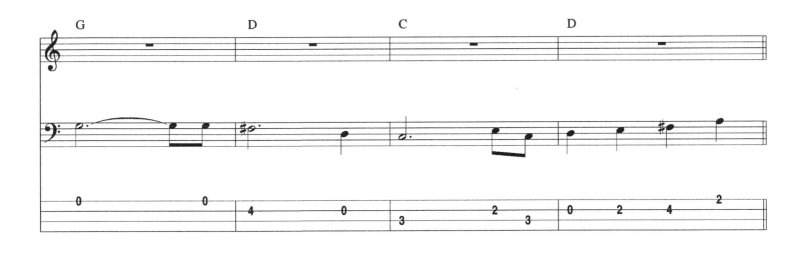

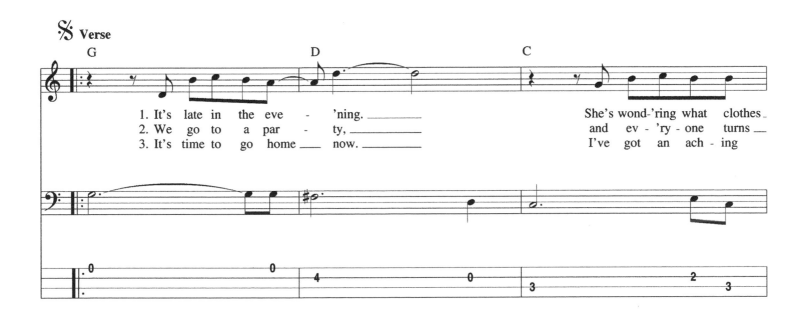

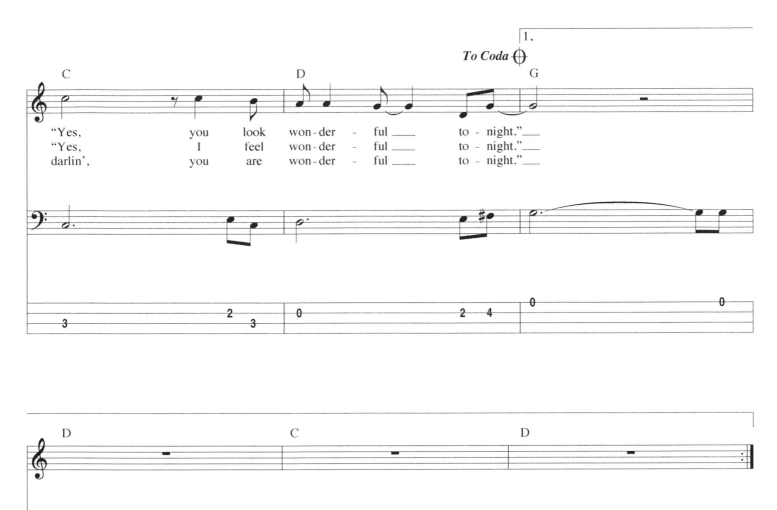

"Yes, you look won-der-ful ___ to - night." ___
"Yes, I feel won-der-ful ___ to - night." ___
darlin', you are won-der-ful ___ to - night." ___

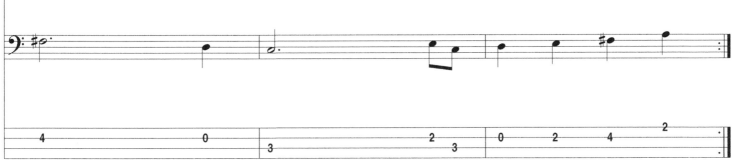

I feel won - der - ful ___ be -

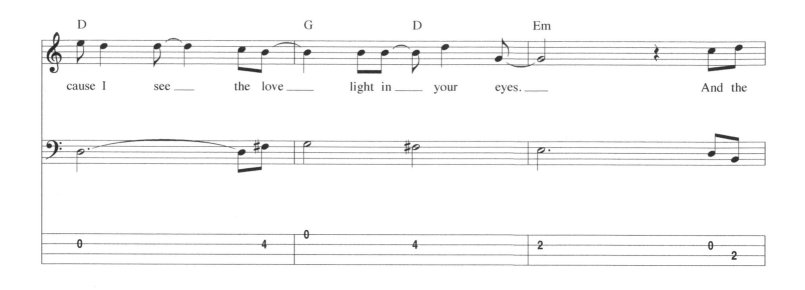

cause I   see ___   the love ___   light in ___ your   eyes. ___   And the

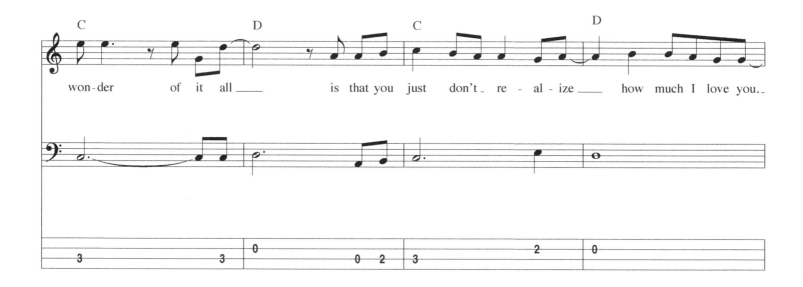

won-der   of it all ___   is that you just   don't _ re - al - ize ___   how much I love you._

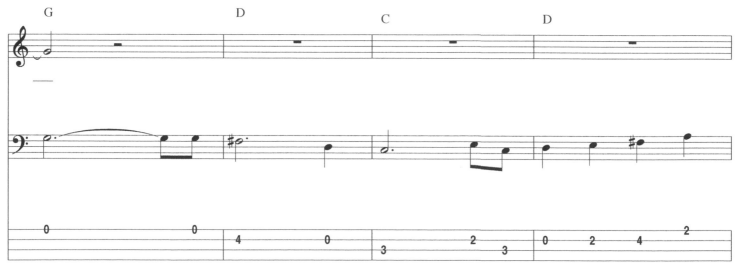

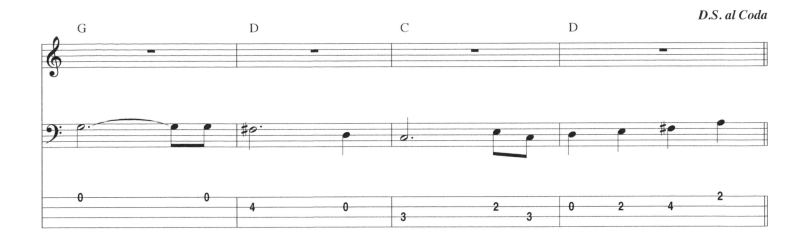

Coda

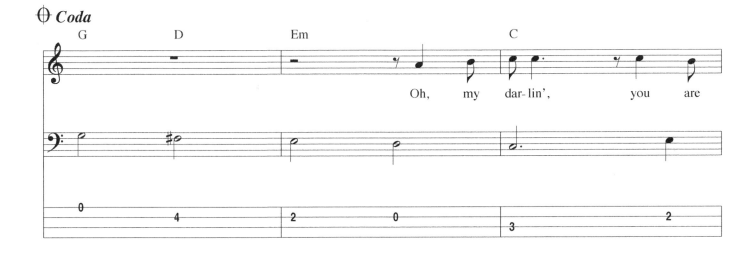

Oh, my dar-lin', you are

Outro

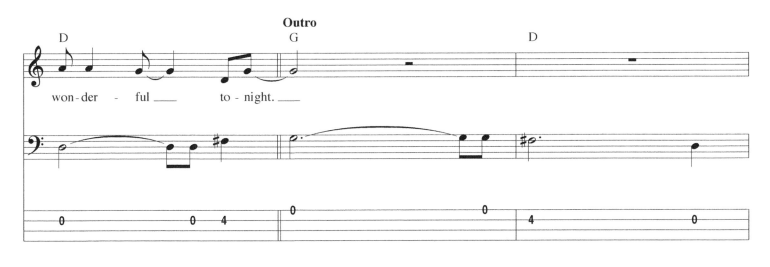

won-der - ful ___ to - night. ___

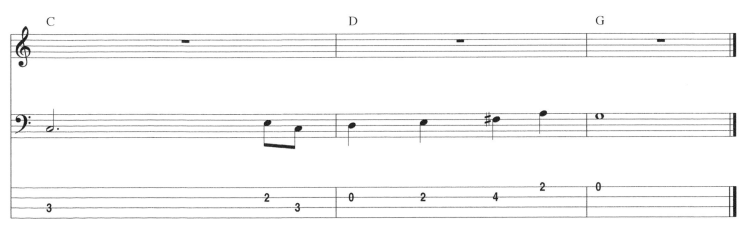

Your Song

Words and Music by Elton John and Bernie Taupin

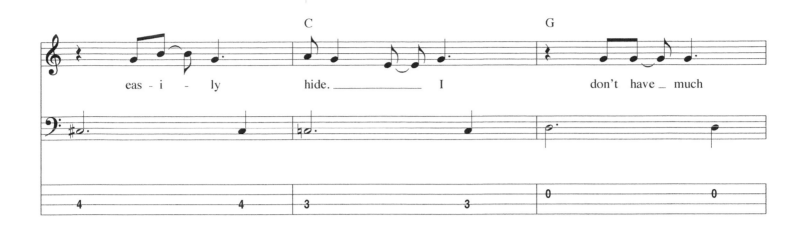

eas - i - ly hide. _____ I don't have _ much

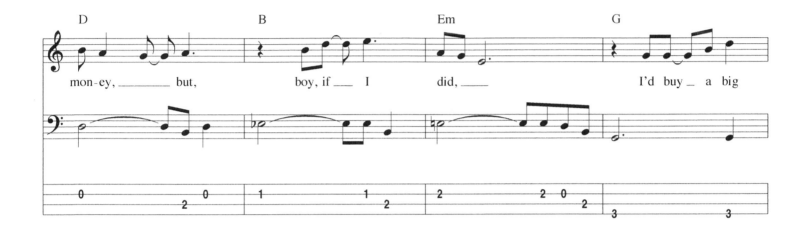

mon-ey, _____ but, boy, if _ I did, _____ I'd buy _ a big

house where ___ we both _ could live.

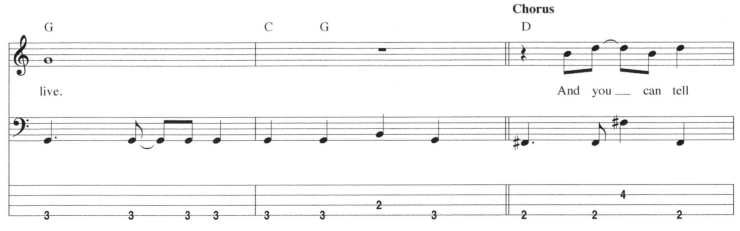

live. And you ___ can tell

Em   Am7   D

ev - 'ry- bod - y   this _ is your   song. ____   It may _ be

Em   Am   C

quite ___ sim - ple, but   now that it's done, _____

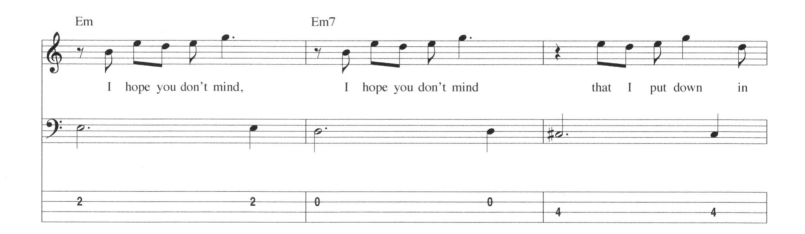

Em   Em7

I hope you don't mind,   I hope you don't mind   that I put down in

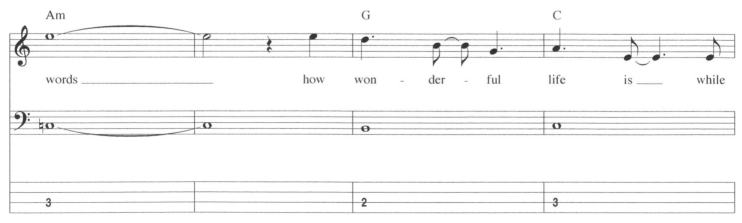

Am   G   C

words _____   how won - der - ful life is ___ while

Outro

life   is ___ while   you're _   in ___ the   world.

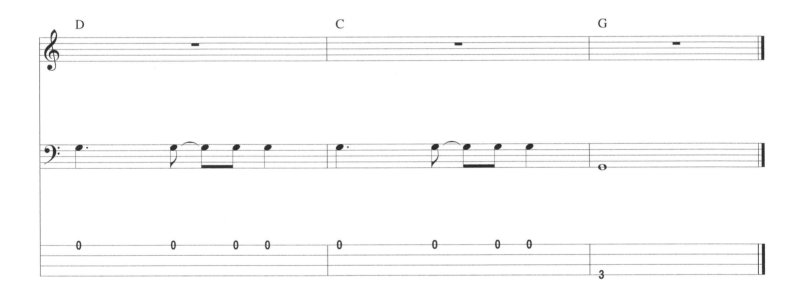

Additional Lyrics

2. If I was a sculptor, but then again no
   or a man who makes potions in a travelin' show…
   I know it's not much, but it's the best I can do.
   My gift is my song and this one's for you.

3. I sat on the roof and kicked off the moss.
   Well, a few of the verses well, they've got me quite cross.
   But the sun's been quite kind while I wrote this song.
   It's for people like you that keep it turned on.

4. So excuse me forgetting, but these things I do.
   You see I've forgotten if they're green, ha, or they're blue.
   Anyway, the thing is, what I really mean,
   Yours are the sweetest eyes I've ever seen.

Oh, Pretty Woman

Words and Music by Roy Orbison and Bill Dees

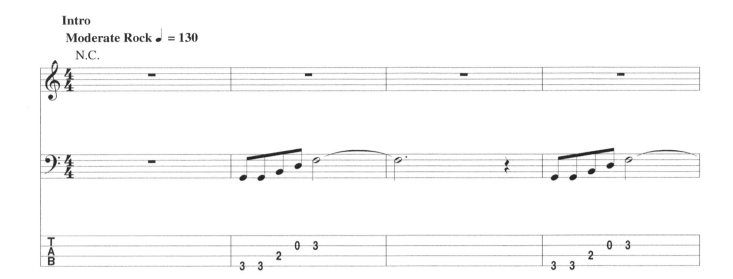

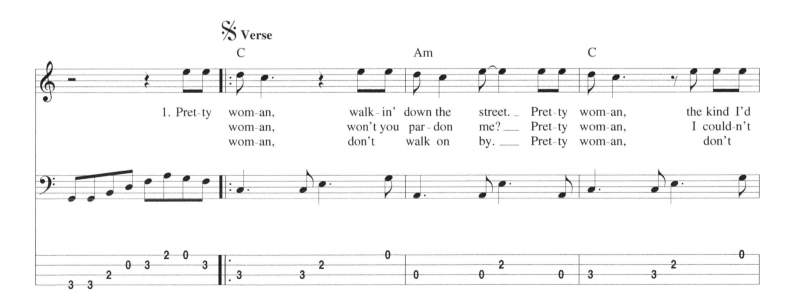

1. Pret-ty wom-an, walk-in' down the street. __ Pret-ty wom-an, the kind I'd
wom-an, won't you par-don me? __ Pret-ty wom-an, I could-n't
wom-an, don't walk on by. __ Pret-ty wom-an, don't

Pret-ty wom - an look my way. _ Pret-ty wom - an, say you'll stay _ with

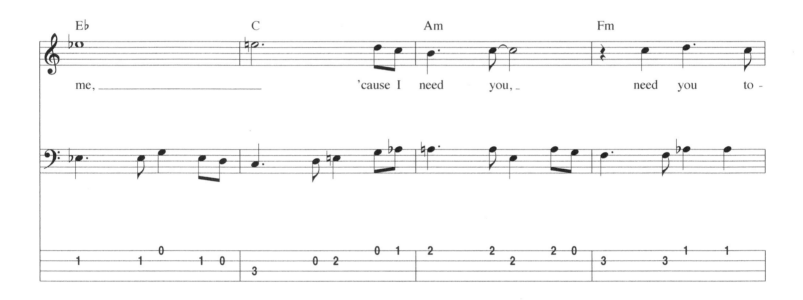

me, _____ 'cause I need you, _ need you to -

night. Come with me, ba - by. _ Be mine to -

N.C.

night. _____ 3. Pret-ty

Coda

G

walk a - way, _____ hey. _____ O. __

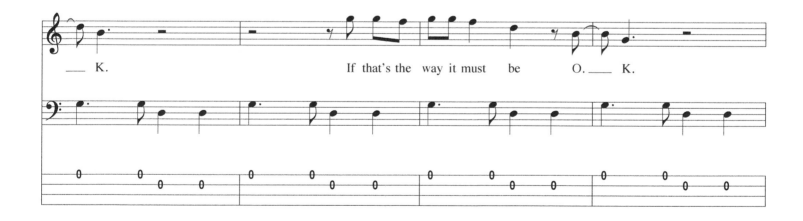

__ K. If that's the way it must be O. __ K.

I guess I'll go on home. __ It's late. ___ There'll be to -

Brown Eyed Girl

Words and Music by Van Morrison

1. Hey where did we ___ go?

2., 3. *See Additional Lyrics*

Days_ when the rains_

33

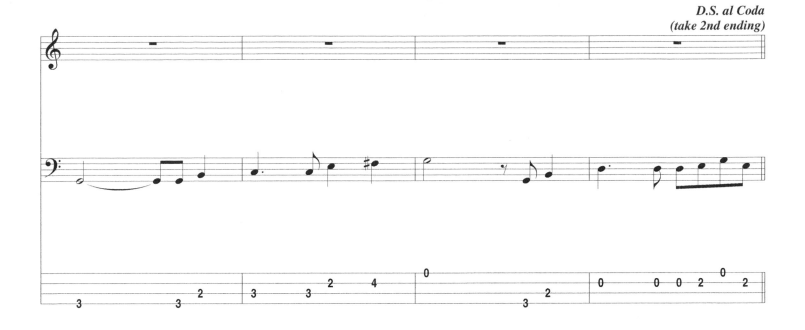

Additional Lyrics

2. Whatever happened to Tuesday and so slow
   Going down the old mine with a transistor radio
   Standing in the sunlight laughing
   Hiding behind a rainbow's wall
   Slipping and a–sliding
   All along the waterfall
   With you, my Brown Eyed Girl.
   You, my Brown Eyed Girl.
   Do you remember when we used to sing:
   Chorus

3. So hard to find my way, now that I'm all on my own
   I saw you just the other day, my, how you have grown
   Cast my memory back there, Lord
   Sometime I'm overcome thinking 'bout
   Making love in the green grass
   Behind the stadium
   With you, my Brown Eyed Girl
   With you, my Brown Eyed Girl.
   Do you remember when we used to sing:
   Chorus

Great Balls of Fire

Words and Music by Otis Blackwell and Jack Hammer

FastTrack is the fastest way for beginners to learn to play the instrument they just bought. **FastTrack** is different from other method books: we've made our book/audio packs user-friendly with plenty of cool songs that make it easy and fun for players to teach themselves. Plus, the last section of the books have the same songs so that students can form a band and jam together. Songbooks for guitar, bass, keyboard and drums are all compatible, and feature eight songs. All packs include great play-along audio with a professional-sounding back-up band.

FastTrack Bass

by Blake Neely & Jeff Schroedl

Level 1
00264732	Method Book/Online Media	$14.99
00697284	Method Book/Online Audio	$7.99
00696404	Method Book/Online Audio + DVD	$14.99
00697289	Songbook 1/Online Audio	$12.99
00695368	Songbook 2/Online Audio	$12.99
00696440	Rock Songbook with CD	$12.99
00696058	DVD	$7.99

Level 2
00697294	Method Book/Online Audio	$9.99
00697298	Songbook 1/Online Audio	$12.99
00695369	Songbook 2/Online Audio	$12.99

FastTrack Drum

by Blake Neely & Rick Mattingly

Level 1
00264733	Method Book/Online Media	$14.99
00697285	Method Book/Online Audio	$7.99
00696405	Method Book/Online Audio + DVD	$14.99
00697290	Songbook 1/Online Audio	$12.99
00695367	Songbook 2/Online Audio	$12.99
00696441	Rock Songbook with CD	$12.99
00696059	DVD	$7.99

Level 2
00697295	Method Book/Online Audio	$9.99
00697299	Songbook 1/Online Audio	$12.99
00695371	Songbook 2/Online Audio	$12.99

FastTrack Guitar
For Electric or Acoustic Guitar, or Both

by Blake Neely & Jeff Schroedl

Level 1
00264731	Method Book/Online Media	$14.99
00697282	Method Book/Online Audio	$7.99
00696403	Method Book/Online Audio + DVD	$14.99
00697287	Songbook 1/Online Audio	$12.99
00695343	Songbook 2/Online Audio	$12.99
00696438	Rock Songbook with CD	$12.99
00696057	DVD	$7.99

Level 2
00697286	Method Book/Online Audio	$9.99
00697296	Songbook/Online Audio	$14.99

Chords & Scales
00697291	Book/Online Audio	$10.99

FastTrack Keyboard
For Electric Keyboard, Synthesizer or Piano

by Blake Neely & Gary Meisner

Level 1
00264734	Method Book/Online Media	$14.99
00697283	Method Book/Online Audio	$7.99
00696406	Method Book/Online Audio + DVD	$14.99
00697288	Songbook 1/Online Audio	$12.99
00696439	Rock Songbook with CD	$12.99
00696060	DVD	$7.99

Level 2
00697293	Method Book/Online Audio	$9.99

Chords & Scales
00697292	Book/Online Audio	$9.99

FastTrack Harmonica

by Blake Neely & Doug Downing

Level 1
00695407	Method Book/Online Audio	$7.99
00695958	Mini Method Book with CD	$7.95
00820016	Mini Method/CD + Harmonica	$12.99
00695574	Songbook/Online Audio	$12.99

Level 2
00695889	Method Book/Online Audio	$9.99
00695891	Songbook with CD	$12.99

FastTrack Lead Singer

by Blake Neely

Level 1
00695408	Method Book/Online Audio	$7.99
00695410	Songbook/Online Audio	$14.99

Level 2
00695890	Method Book/Online Audio	$9.95
00695892	Songbook with CD	$12.95

FastTrack Saxophone

by Blake Neely

Level 1
00695241	Method Book/Online Audio	$7.99
00695409	Songbook/Online Audio	$14.99

FastTrack Ukulele

by Chad Johnson

Level 1
00114417	Method Book/Online Audio	$7.99
00158671	Songbook/Online Audio	$12.99

Level 2
00275508	Method Book/Online Audio	$9.99

FastTrack Violin

by Patrick Clark

Level 1
00141262	Method Book/Online Audio	$7.99

HAL•LEONARD®

Visit Hal Leonard online at **www.halleonard.com**

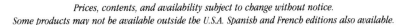

HAL•LEONARD® BASS PLAY-ALONG

The Bass Play-Along™ Series will help you play your favorite songs quickly and easily! Just follow the tab, listen to the audio to hear how the bass should sound, and then play-along using the separate backing tracks. The melody and lyrics are also included in the book in case you want to sing, or to simply help you follow along. The audio files are enhanced so you can adjust the recording to any tempo without changing pitch!

HAL•LEONARD®

Prices, contents, and availability subject to change without notice.

Visit Hal Leonard Online at **www.halleonard.com**